Original title:
Lost Among Leaves

Copyright © 2025 Creative Arts Management OÜ
All rights reserved.

Author: Adrian Caldwell
ISBN HARDBACK: 978-1-80567-177-0
ISBN PAPERBACK: 978-1-80567-476-4

Glimmers of Gold in the Gloom

In the woods where shadows creep,
Napped a squirrel, in dreams so deep.
Chasing acorns, he took a leap,
Now he's tangled in a heap.

Twigs and branches all around,
He yelps a bit, then looks quite proud.
With golden leaves as his crown,
He struts about, like a circus clown.

Beneath the Undergrowth's Solitude

A turtle wearing shoes so bright,
Took a stroll, oh what a sight!
Thought he'd dance, oh what a plight,
His little feet took flight—then blight.

Beneath the ferns, a party grew,
With bugs and frogs, who knew what to do.
They grooved along, in a leafy hue,
While our turtle tripped—who even knew?

Whispers in the Canopy

The leaves all gossip, soft and sly,
As the raccoon waves, oh my, oh my!
"Is that a snack?" he asks the sky,
And tumbles down with a comical sigh.

A cheeky bird, with a beak so bright,
Sings a tune, quite out of sight.
In the treetop party, they take flight,
Making mischief till the night.

Dance of the Fallen

A pile of leaves, so crunchy and neat,
Where bunnies hop, to the beat.
They jig and whirl with little feet,
Life's a stage, isn't it sweet?

The wind joins in, with a giggle and swirl,
As twirling leaves start to twirl and hurl.
The critters cheer, in a wild whirl,
Nature's dance—give it a twirl!

The Rustle of Hidden Secrets

In the garden, whispers play,
A squirrel drops his acorn ballet.
The breeze laughs, a ticklish tease,
While ants march on with daring ease.

Frogs join in a croaky song,
Singing notes that feel so wrong.
The daisies giggle with delight,
As butterflies take off in flight.

Mosaics of Nature's Abandon

A patch of grass, a hidden seat,
Where ladybugs set up their meet.
The sunbeam shines, a prankster's grin,
As whispers win, and giggles spin.

The oak tree winks, a cheeky mime,
Swaying branches in perfect rhyme.
Old leaves drop for a quick surprise,
As squirrels scamper, oh, how time flies!

A Journey Through Time's Green Veil

Beneath the boughs, the gnomes convene,
Planning pranks that are quite unseen.
The wind hums tunes of days gone by,
As pine cones take off for a sky-high fly.

A beetle struts in shiny pride,
While mushrooms giggle, can't let slide.
A rustle here, a titter there,
Nature's plot thickens, if you dare!

Threads of Nature's Enchantment

The spider weaves a silly plan,
A disco ball for every man.
Bumblebees buzz, a lively crew,
Planning dance-offs, if you only knew!

The bushes shiver, secrets shared,
As onlookers gasp, completely bared.
With every hop and rustle near,
The forest laughs, oh what a cheer!

Embracing the Decay

In a pile of brown, I sit and sigh,
Wondering where all the green did fly.
A squirrel mocks me with acorn stocks,
While I play hide and seek with my socks.

The branches creak like a rickety joke,
As I try to float on a leaf like a boat.
But the wind's a prankster, a playful tease,
I land on my face, dignity on freeze.

Remnants of the Rich Canopy

Once clothed in green, now a patchy quilt,
I navigate through the remnants built.
An owl hoots, 'Hey, what's up with you?'
As I trip on roots in my clumsy shoe.

A twig snaps loud, like thunder's roar,
I jump in fright; it's the bush's chore.
But a squirrel brings snacks, a hidden delight,
While I chuckle softly through the leafy bite.

Chronicles of Chlorophyll

The stories told by each twisted vine,
Remind me of days when the sun would shine.
Now I'm writing with ink from a berry's heart,
Too bad it stains, and I'm like a work of art.

I meet a beetle, a spy in disguise,
With tiny binoculars, oh, what a surprise!
We gossip of leaves and secretive flights,
While ants form a band, with drums in the nights.

Twilight in the Thicket

As shadows stretch in a playful dance,
I juggle with fireflies, giving them a chance.
A raccoon winks, sharing tales of the dusk,
Teaching me fortune in muffin crumbs' husk.

I flip through the thicket, like a wild book,
Where every page is a peek and a look.
With laughter and rustles, a melodic spree,
I find joy in nature's delightful decree.

Shadows in the Underbrush

Squirrels in acorns, a nutty parade,
Jumping and tumbling, oh, such a charade.
A raccoon in the shadow, peeking at me,
Wearing a mask like it's Halloween spree.

Frogs in the puddles, croaking their song,
Challenging crickets, they think they're so strong.
A leaf on my head, I adjust it with flair,
Nature's new fashion, I'm a woodland bear.

The ants form a line, they're marching in sync,
Carrying crumbs, a picnic, I think.
A deer with a twinkle, gazes so shy,
Winks at the laugh, then continues to fly.

Underbrush whispers, a chuckle or two,
The trees laugh together, in a green-golden hue.
With giggles and tickles, the forest awakes,
In the shadows it dances, as joy overtakes.

Echoes of the Woodland

In the canopy, giggles of folks,
With owls and raccoons sharing their jokes.
"Why did the bear wear a frisbee today?"
"Because it wasn't quite ready for play!"

Bluejays perform in their feathered attire,
Practicing ballet, they leap and they tire.
A squirrel takes a bow, all fluffy and grand,
Nuts fly like confetti, it's quite a demand.

Mossy green carpets, a stage set for fun,
Where hedgehogs roll in a race just begun.
Wobbling and bobbling, they tumble and roll,
Even the toads join, it's a wild, funny stroll.

Echoes of laughter, dance through the trees,
Nature's comedians, putting hearts at ease.
With whispers of joy that tickle the ground,
The woodland sings out, a playful surround.

The Secret Beneath the Boughs

Underneath branches, whispers collide,
Where chipmunks tell tales, with nowhere to hide.
Secrets in shadows, a giggle or snort,
Owls with their glasses, missed their report!

Moles throw a party, under the soil,
Dancing and laughing, their antics uncoil.
With cupcakes and dirt, they feast like the kings,
In miniature castles, they enjoy tiny things.

A rabbit in bowtie takes center stage,
Telling jokes that would make any critter rage.
"If you can't hop high, just wiggle your nose,"
A chorus of laughter, the forest then grows.

Under the boughs, when night starts to creep,
The woodland reveals its delightful sweep.
With chuckles and murmurs that flutter and fly,
Nature keeps secrets beneath the night sky.

Veiled in Verdant Silence

In the emerald maze, where chuckles retreat,
A hedgehog is plotting, with hoots, how sweet!
Giggling grass blades join in the spree,
Whispering tales of the buzzing bee.

Worms hold debates on the softness of earth,
While lilies giggle, they're just having mirth.
A snail on a mission, so slow, oh so slick,
Thinks he's a racer, but takes it for kicks.

Even the mushrooms lean in for the show,
With caps that are laughing, all aglow.
"Why don't you wiggle and dance and get down?"
Said a butterfly wearing a glittering crown.

Veils of green laughter, in shadows, they twirl,
The dance of the forest, a whimsical whirl.
In this delightful silence, the joy doesn't cease,
As nature spins stories, it hugs us in peace.

In the Embrace of Earth's Canopy

Beneath the branches, shadows dance,
I tripped on roots while chasing chance.
The squirrels laughed, they knew my fate,
As I tangled up, I was their bait.

The sunbeams peek through leafy dreams,
I thought I'd stroll, but how it seems,
A secret path, now I'm the jest,
A wanderer in nature's quest.

With every step, a slip, a slide,
The forest giggles, what a ride!
I sought direction, found a vine,
A swing of green, I'm feeling fine.

In the embrace of verdant cheer,
My map was wrong, but who needs sheer?
With nature's humor all around,
I dance with trees; I'm glory bound!

The Veil of Time in the Forest

A clock made of wood ticks not at all,
While I'm lost in leaves, hear nature's call.
The ferns are nodding, wise and spry,
Where did I put my phone? Oh my.

The past is a whisper all around,
The acorn falls, the lost are found.
In tangles of ivy, I trip and roll,
Just a moment to ponder, what's my goal?

I ran with rabbits, they questioned my style,
Told me to hop, and stay for a while.
With each little giggle, I chuckle and sway,
Time blooms like daisies, in the funniest way.

So here's to the forest, its quirks and charms,
Where trees have secrets, and nature disarms.
Through laughter and wonder, I wander free,
In this veil of time, I'm just being me!

Treetop Reveries

Up in the branches, the view is grand,
But my trusty hat flew from my hand.
The birds are mocking, with chirps so bold,
As I reach for my headgear, brave yet sold.

A rope swing beckons, I take the leap,
Navigate twigs like a child, not deep.
With laughter unleashed like a wild breeze,
I swirl around like a swarm of bees.

The raccoons peek from their leafy nooks,
While I read their faces like storybooks.
Caught in this moment, a giggle parade,
Through treetops I drift, in the joy I've made.

Nature's a jester, it tickles my soul,
I swing through canopies, that's my goal.
With friends made of feathers and bark, oh dear,
In these treetop reveries, I center my cheer!

Enigma in the Lush Archway

Here I stand beneath leafy arches,
Lost in puzzle paths, where my heart marches.
Every twist a riddle, every root a clue,
With a map made of dreams, who knew it was true?

In secret glades, I strike a pose,
The ferns erupt with laughter, who knows?
I twirl like a leaf, in a dizzy spree,
Nature's mystery unfolding, just for me.

A squirrel names me the forest's queen,
While a toad serenades with a woozy tune.
Laughter erupts, from the creek to the sky,
In this enigma, I'm no longer shy.

So here I wander, the forest's delight,
With whispers of whimsy, I dance through the light.
An archway of laughter, trees waving near,
In this lush mystery, I'm grinning ear to ear!

The Dance of the Fading Sunlight

The sun slips down, a clumsy clown,
Tripping on branches, wearing a frown.
It dances with shadows, a goofy tease,
Swinging to rhythms of rustling leaves.

With every twirl, the squirrels sigh,
'Look at that sunlight, he's about to fly!'
The grass giggles, a bright green best,
As the twilight shines on this light-hearted jest.

A chipmunk claps, the audience wild,
While fireflies flash, like stars, so beguiled.
The tree trunks sway, a gentle cheer,
For the sun, our jester, that draws ever near.

Secrets Intertwined with Roots

Beneath the soil, secrets huddle tight,
Where ants host tea parties, what a sight!
They gossip of woodland, and mushrooms abloom,
While tree roots dance in a tangled room.

A squirrel joins in, its cheeks puffed out,
'What's hot in the woods? Do tell me, no doubt!'
They giggle and chatter, in leafy attire,
As evening creeps in, like a sly little liar.

The roots share tales, both grand and bizarre,
Of owls who serenade, beneath the night star.
While the wind, in jest, whispers sweet nothings,
And the branches burst out in playful strumming.

Echoes of the Whispering Wild

In the wild, the echoes call out,
'Meet us for tea and a cheeky shout!'
A deer wears a scarf, with a wink so sly,
While rabbits play hopscotch, oh my, oh my!

The wind tells jokes with a gusty grin,
Rustling the leaves, beneath every skin.
A bear in a hat juggles fruits from a tree,
Shouting, 'Catch, if you wish to be free!'

There's laughter aplenty, in the bright sunny glade,
A chorus of chirps, like a band of parade.
The wild stands united, in joy and in jest,
Celebrating nature, feeling so blessed.

Forgotten Trails of Wood and Wind

On forgotten trails, where the whispers play,
The wind tells secrets from far away.
Moss cushions laughter, on footsteps of old,
While tickling the toes of the trolls' hidden gold.

A fox in a waistcoat recites poems to trees,
Dancing in circles, as chattering bees.
The paths twist and turn, like a comedy skit,
Where the roots crack jokes, and the branches submit.

A chorus of crickets joins in the fun,
As the sun sets low, giving way to the pun.
The forest erupts, in a jovial spree,
Where every creature finds joy, just to be free.

Whispers of Autumn's Embrace

With squirrels sporting tiny hats,
And acorns rolling like baseball bats,
The trees giggle as branches sway,
While foolish deer come out to play.

A leaf fell down and bumped my nose,
I swore it grumbled, 'Watch out, doze!'
A gust of wind said, 'Catch me now!'
But I tripped over a rogue cow.

The pumpkins wink with mischief bright,
While owls hoot jokes in the fading light.
The chilly air plays hide and seek,
And golden skies are far from bleak.

When twilight falls, the woods conspire,
To dance and twirl with giddy fire.
Oh autumn, with your playful tease,
You bring such joy—just don't sneeze!

Shadows of the Fallen Canopy

Beneath the trees where shadows creep,
The raccoons plot their midnight leap.
A pumpkin spice latte in hand,
It's the perfect spot for a jesting band.

Chasing shadows, my friends declare,
'Is that a ghost or just old hair?'
We giggle at the snapping twigs,
While squirrels run about like prancing jigs.

Leaves rustle secrets, whispers wane,
The wind joins in with a hearty strain.
A branch sways low, almost to tease,
I duck and dodge, whoa—watch those knees!

With all this fun, who needs a plan?
The woods unfold with a jovial span.
So let's embrace this leafy cheer,
And laugh as nature draws us near.

In the Arms of Nature's Decay

In cozy piles, the leaves are stacked,
They whisper tales of how they cracked.
The pumpkins grin with crooked smiles,
While critters dance in fanciful piles.

A snail in boots, oh what a sight!
Claims he'll win the great leaf flight.
With laughter ringing all around,
Even the mushrooms wiggle on the ground.

Oh what a mess, this autumn scene,
With toadstools wearing hats of green.
The breeze just chuckles, a knowing sort,
As daisies giggle, 'What a sport!'

So come and gather, fresh air awaits,
To join this romp through twisting gates.
For in decay, we find delight,
Let laughter bloom in autumn's light.

Echoes Beneath the Branches

Under branches where shadows flop,
The squirrels dare each other to stop.
'Bet you can't leap from this tall pine!'
As acorns plummet, they laugh—divine.

A grasshopper sings with melodies grand,
His tune drowns out the nearby band.
The breeze blows soft, a playful jest,
As critters settle for their nest.

Beneath the trees, it seems quite clear,
That autumn's world is full of cheer.
With every crunch beneath our feet,
We waltz through trails, oh what a treat!

So let's rejoice with twirls and spins,
In this playground where laughter begins.
Each echo resonates with glee,
As nature dances, wild and free.

When Time Stands Still in the Woods

Squirrels argue over acorns,
One claims it's a treasure map,
While birds laugh in the branches,
Sipping tea from a floppy hat.

Frogs in robes host a ballet,
Dancing on lily pads with flair,
A bear joins in, but his moves,
Are more of a clumsy bear stare.

Sunbeams peek in curiously,
Tickling the ferns, oh so bright,
The shadows play hide and seek,
While the mushrooms just hold tight.

And if you hear a soft giggle,
It's likely a leaf getting teased,
Each time the wind starts to rustle,
Nature's laughter is released.

The Quietude of Golden Fragments

A leaf fell down with a splat,
It mistook the ground for a seat,
Grumpy worms had a meeting,
On this hilarious, furrowed street.

A chipmunk tried on a hat,
Made of fluffy marshmallow fluff,
He trotted like a tiny king,
As squirrels called, 'That's quite enough!'

Sunsets drip like ice cream cones,
All the colors ran a race,
The clouds whispered silly secrets,
As they took on a pink embrace.

In this corner of humor,
Nature wears a dazzling grin,
Even the crickets chuckle soft,
As twilight settles in thin.

Beneath the Rustling Canopy

Below the trees, a party thrived,
With twirling ants in funky shoes,
They served nut pies and berry juice,
While a hedgehog sang the blues.

A turtle juggled acorns bright,
While chatting with a bingeing mouse,
The ladybugs took flight for fun,
Crammed in a tiny, painted house.

The wind raced by, swept up the leaves,
A carousel that spun with cheer,
Branches shook in playful jest,
Ticking time off, year by year.

But every so often, hush now,
Listen for the giggles loud,
Even the owls wink knowingly,
At the antics of their leafy crowd.

Tales Woven in the Wind

Once, a gust brought a joke so grand,
A bumblebee tried stand-up flair,
But all that buzz made folks roll eyes,
Still, the flowers welcomed him there.

A pair of frogs in bow ties stood,
On a rock, giving slick advice,
Their wisdom wrapped in silly puns,
It seemed like nature's own device.

Leaves fluttered down like whispers sweet,
Sharing secrets, tales untold,
In the distance, a deer snickered,
Watching the antics bold.

Laughter echoed through the thicket,
Every rustle brought new delight,
Nature's jesters, in full swing,
Keep the woodland mood so bright.

The Dance of Dappled Light

In sunlight's warm, playful embrace,
The shadows twirl at a lively pace.
A squirrel spins, does a cheeky twirl,
While branches bob in a leafy whirl.

The bugs join in, with a buzzing cheer,
Oh, how the trees wish they could appear!
With branches outstretched, they laugh and sway,
As rabbits jump into the fray.

Beneath the beams, the critters convene,
A joyous jam, quite the silly scene.
The sunlight flickers, on stage they prance,
A comedy of shadows, a light-hearted dance.

Forgotten Footsteps on Leafy Paths

A path of crunch with every stride,
Yet who knew that shoes tend to hide?
With hidden stones and pesky twigs,
These footloose trips turn into digs!

Where did I leave those silly flats?
I trip on roots and chat with bats.
Each step's a giggle, a fall, a hop,
Nature's laughter makes my heart pop!

With muddy socks and flapping shoes,
The trail informs me of my lost clues.
Silly me, how did I wander?
Oh look, the woods have brought me wonder!

Secrets Beneath the Forest Floor

What mysteries lie beneath the ground?
A family of gnomes, or perhaps a mound?
The roots curl tightly, a ticklish tale,
They rise in laughter, in leafy detail.

With acorns bobbing like little boats,
The earthworms claim their pasta coats.
A snail sings softly, in slimy glee,
While secrets of soil dance quietly.

Beneath the layers, a world does bloom,
A raucous party held in gloom.
The mushrooms giggle as pitchers pout,
In this underground bar, there's no doubt!

A Tapestry of Color and Silence

A patch of colors, oh what a sight,
Leaves whisper secrets in sheer delight.
A butterfly flutters, gossiping bends,
While squirrels exchange their soft, silly trends.

The reds and golds swap winks and glares,
Each shade a story in nature's airs.
In quiet corners, the colors lie,
Mimicking giggles from passersby.

With paintbrushes made of dappled light,
They giggle at dusk, a comedic plight.
A canvas alive, with jokes and song,
In this vibrant realm, nothing feels wrong!

The Sound of Silence Beneath the Trees

Squirrels chattered, quite a thrill,
While I stumbled, drank my fill.
Nature giggled, what a scene,
Me tripping over roots so green.

Branches whispered, secrets told,
As I searched for snacks—oh so bold!
A crow cawed, saying 'Hey, look here!'
I waved back, pretending to cheer.

Beneath the shade, I took my nap,
Dreaming of snacks, a lovely trap.
Leaves overheard my yummy schemes,
And laughed out loud, or so it seems.

Sunlight danced with gentle rays,
While I wandered in a daze.
The woods, a stage for comic antics,
Nature's humor—so gigantic!

Reflections of a Wistful Wanderer

In the woods, I lost my way,
Hoping to find a snack today.
Branches laughed as I passed by,
I gave a wink, not knowing why.

The brook babbled, 'You look fine!'
I curtsied back, sipping brine.
Mushrooms giggled, pointing out,
'Is that your shoe? Or a potato sprout?'

With every step, the laughter grew,
Leaves whispered jokes for me and you.
I tripped and fell—oh what a sight!
Nature rolled its eyes in delight.

Yet in this comedy, I found my peace,
Wandering here, my worries cease.
Each tumble, each chuckle, brightens the day,
Amidst the trees where humor plays.

Seasons Gone, Leaves Turned

Autumn breezes played their tune,
Dancing leaves beneath the moon.
I chased a leaf, oh what a race,
Tripped on a twig—oh, what a face!

The trees chuckled, swayed with glee,
While I giggled at a bumblebee.
'Catch me if you can!' the leaf did tease,
As I stumbled down, skirting trees.

Pinecones tumbled, oh such fun,
A game of dodge; I could not run.
I laughed so hard, the wind did sigh,
'Some things never change; oh my, oh my!'

Seasons shift, but joy stays true,
In every laugh, the trees renew.
So I embrace the silly show,
Among the branches, happiness will grow.

Traces of a Fading Journey

A path well-worn, or was it new?
I waved to ants, they waved back too.
Kicked a rock, danced down the lane,
Where did I leave my brain again?

Whispers of grass beneath my feet,
Nature chuckled, what a treat!
My compass spun like a dizzy bee,
Each step a joke; oh, woe is me!

Clouds above began to tease,
I waved at them, and told them, 'Please!'
They laughed out loud, a rainy cheer,
Puddles formed, now let's not steer.

A journey halted for laughs so bright,
In nature's grip, I found delight.
With every step, the laughter stayed,
Traces of joy in the mess I've made.

Serenade of Crumbling Petals

Once I danced with the breeze's tune,
But tripped on petals, oh what a swoon!
The flowers giggled, a cheeky sight,
Where blooms turn to crumbs in the fading light.

With every step, a crunch in the air,
I laughed at the mess with floral flair.
Nature's confetti, oh what a show,
At my feet, petals spun in a row.

The bees all buzzed, in laughter they flew,
A banquet of blossoms, they knew what to do.
My two left feet, a comical feat,
In the garden's chaos, I admit defeat.

Yet I twirled through the remnants, carefree and bold,
In this petal parade, I found glimmers of gold.
So if you see me, a clumsy ballet,
Just join in the fun, let's dance the day away!

Autumn's Solitude

In a pile of leaves, I took my seat,
Squirrels stared back, the woodland elite.
I waved at a tree, it gave a slow sigh,
I'm not alone here, just me and the sky.

The crunch of the foliage, a crackling tune,
I swear that one leaf is a miniature moon.
With acorns a-falling, they're clattering down,
Is that nature's way of making a crown?

A crow nearby cawed, it sounded like laughter,
I told him my woes, but he just flew after.
He squawked and he flopped, I felt quite a fool,
In this autumnal mess, who needs a rule?

With each gust of wind, I twirled in delight,
Embracing the chaos, I flew like a kite.
So if you find me, just me and my cheer,
Join in the leaves, the laughter is near!

The Lace of Afterthought

There's a lace on the ground, what a curious thing,
A delicate covering where fairies might sing.
But as I bent down, I slipped on a vine,
This tricky embroidery, oh, how it's divine!

My mind started wandering, oh where did it go?
Tangled in wonders, like roots in the snow.
I giggled and stumbled, a graceful dismay,
The lace of my thoughts had all gone astray.

Amongst the bright colors, I tripped on some moss,
A dance of confusion, the trees had a gloss.
Is this a garden or a circus parade?
With giggles and tumbles, the line starts to fade.

So if you are lost in laces today,
Remember to laugh, let the mischief play.
The twirling of leaves is a fine, jolly sight,
In the lace of my thoughts, I take wondrous flight!

Driftwood and Dust

On driftwood I sat, a beach bum supreme,
With sand in my shorts, oh where is the dream?
The waves rolled in laughter, as I made a mess,
In such sticky situations, I must confess.

A seagull swooped down, snatched fries from my hand,
I waved it goodbye, my lunch stolen by sand.
With grains in my toes and salt in my hair,
I laughed at the wind like it just didn't care.

The sun slipped away, a slippery slide,
Misty dreams mingled with laughter and tide.
The twilight chuckled, casting shadows so bright,
With driftwood and dust, my heart took to flight.

So if you're out wandering, embrace every gust,
In the wood and the waves, find joy in the rust.
Let waves tickle your toes, giggle with glee,
For in every grain found, there's a tale just for thee!

On the Edge of a Rustling Memory

In a forest where squirrels conspire,
A dance of twigs creates laughter,
A squirrel stole my sandwich, oh the liar!
He nibbled and scurried, chasing disaster.

With leaves like confetti, winds play around,
A picnic disrupted makes quite the tale,
While I chased the thief, no sandwich I found,
But the birds cheered me on, their chirps like a gale.

Every rustle a giggle, the trees join with glee,
They chuckle at my plight, their leaves in spree,
For nature's a joker with tricks up her sleeve,
And I'm the jester, so it seems to be!

So next time you wander and hear a soft sound,
Beware of the critters who play on the ground,
For laughter's the echo, in each leafy caress,
And sometimes, the forest brings pure silliness!

The Poetry of Drifting Leaves

A leaf landed softly atop my head,
A hat made of ochre, quite the fine mix,
I strutted like royalty, things that I said,
Until a gust stole my crown, what a fix!

The trees giggled softly, their voices so light,
A parade of leaves danced by my side,
I joined in their frolic, oh what a sight,
But tripped on a twig, my dignity died.

Every tumble and twirl, a new comical scene,
As I rolled like a tumbleweed, trying to flee,
The sun peeked down, it knew I was keen,
Laughter erupted; it was wild and free!

The poetry whispered through branches above,
In the crunch of each leaf, a rhythm and beat,
So when you hear nature's giggle of love,
Join in the jest; let your heart skip a beat!

Through the Veil of Fall's Edition

In a world dipped in gold, the trees told their tales,
Of mishaps and mischief that danced on the breeze,
With each crunching step, they shared their old fails,
As I strolled through this canvas, I couldn't appease.

A slippery acorn, a twist, and a glide,
I splashed into piles like a leaf-covered clown,
The squirrels were cackling, my dignity fried,
While a nearby crow just sang, 'Look at that clown!'

With shadows of laughter, the sun had a smile,
Each crumb of the earth chuckled underfoot,
I'd join in their antics, but oh it's a trial,
To stay upright in nature's delightful pursuit!

So here's to the folly, the joy in the fall,
The whispers of wisdom that tickle the ground,
For in every misstep, laughter's the call,
And folly brings friends where the fun can be found!

A Symphony of Color and Sorrow

A symphony played with a rustling sound,
Browns, reds, and yellows in nature's ballet,
But watch where you step; oh, what might be found,
A slip or a tumble sends humor our way!

The leaves like confetti dance high in the air,
A waltz with the wind, oh what joy they display,
Yet down on the ground? Well, it's quite a scare,
For tripping on nature is my game for today!

The trees are my audience, they nod as I swoon,
While critters applaud with a flurry of cheer,
Each tumble and roll, a comedy tune,
Makes my mishaps feel lighter, oh how they endear!

So here's to the laughter that swirls all around,
In every bright leaf, a memory made,
For symphonies played in each rustling sound,
Are just nature's way to keep joy on parade!

Pathways of the Abandoned

In a park so wild and free,
A squirrel stashed lunch - oh, my knee!
Dodging nuts and plots, oh dear,
Who knew this path could cause such fear?

Wandering aimlessly with rhymes,
My friend just tripped over last year's chimes.
We laugh till we can hardly stand,
As leaves perform a funny band.

Each step we take is fraught with dread,
Watch out for hats that have long fled!
A crow caws at our just-formed dance,
In the maze of leaves, we've lost our chance!

But what's this giggle in the air?
It might just be a leaf's bold dare.
With each gust, we roll and slide,
In this joyful mess, we just abide.

Secrets of the Shifting Shade

Beneath the trees, I spy a thing,
Is it a branch or a rubber ring?
A leaf with jokes, it starts to tease,
Vowing to bounce away with ease!

Under the shadows, whispers giggle,
A pumpkin's grin gives me a wiggle.
One foot slips, my balance unravels,
I tumble forth, facing new travels!

Squirrels start their sneaky chatter,
Are they plotting? Oh, what's the matter?
In this secret, twisted knoll,
I find my laughter, my heart it stole!

The shade shifts, the sun peeks near,
What's that? A bold raccoon in gear!
He's got a hat that's way too grand,
In this leafy cauldron, oh, isn't it grand!

Hushed Revelations of Autumn

In silence thick like jam on bread,
I tiptoe past the trees' wide spread.
A leaf giggles, then flips with glee,
"Catch me if you can!" it calls to me!

Beneath the crunch of amber floor,
I stumble through a leafy door.
With every step, a chuckle blooms,
As whispers follow and fill the rooms!

A hedgehog darts; it's quite a sight,
Wearing a crown that's just not right!
"Is autumn here?" I hear him moan,
"For all I know, I'm still alone!"

But laughter echoes in the bramble,
As I lose my way, it's just a gamble.
Those hushed tales of humor bloom wide,
In autumn's grip, we all just glide!

The Color of Forgotten Moments

In hues of orange and yellow swirl,
Forgotten pies begin to twirl.
Such antics from a pie's sweet crust,
When hungry squirrels stir up a fuss!

The apples giggle, ripe and round,
With tales of pranks that they have found.
A caramel drizzle gone awry,
Beware the sweetness, they all cry!

Under the roof of bending branches,
I contest with leaves and their sly dances.
Each crunch releases a small delight,
Nature's laughter in plain sight!

Ramble forth through this colorful scene,
As pumpkins jive in the air so keen.
The moments here, with giggles bright,
Transform the dark into pure light!

The Journey Through Nature's Lament

A squirrel stole my sandwich today,
I chased him down, what a funny display!
He danced on a branch, all full of glee,
While I stood below, just wondering, 'Why me?'

The trees giggled softly, swaying their heads,
As I tangled my feet in the long leafy spreads.
A rabbit hopped by, gave me a grin,
And off he darted, my patience wore thin.

A crow flew above like a dark little cloud,
Squawking his laughter, he felt oh so proud.
I waved up my hands, yelled, "Hey, what's the deal?"
He cawed louder still, it hurt my ears' appeal.

Thus I sat on the ground, in a nature-filled haze,
Feeling the wonders of these silly days.
With squirrels and crows, and a bunny or two,
Nature's antics had me laughing, it's true!

Embracing the Shifting Tides of Green

The leaves are all dancing, oh what a scene,
With gusty breezes, they seem so serene.
A ladybug waltzes with such little grace,
I clap and I cheer at her colorful race.

There's a frog in a puddle, a prince in disguise,
He croaks out a tune, oh how it complies!
The wind whispers secrets of snails on parade,
While I giggle at squirrels throwing shade—palm made.

In the woods there's a picnic laid out by whim,
But ants had a party, my lunch looked so grim.
I tried to protest, but they all took a row,
Now my granola bar's a buffet, who knew how!

In this ever-shifting green, life is quite odd,
With creatures who prance and leaves that applaud.
Laughter's the banner, waving bright on this ride,
Through nature's own jest, I'm happy to glide!

Reflections in a Blanket of Earth

On the ground lies a puddle, a mirror so round,
I peek in to find a face that's quite clown-bound.
A worm gives a wink, with a squirmy, sly sass,
I chuckle and think, 'Do I resemble that mass?'

A nearby acorn rolled, making quite the sound,
It startled a chipmunk, who jumped all around.
He fell in a heap, then shook off his pride,
While I laughed out loud, can't keep humor inside!

The sun filters down, adding charm to the theme,
Bugs buzzing along, they're all part of the dream.
With dandelions giggling, who could ever frown?
In this world full of jesters, I'm never let down.

Nestled in laughter, on earth's cozy lap,
Nature's a comic, with every mishap.
Through giggles and jests, we dance all around,
Joined by the humor that's blissfully found!

Reverie of the Woodland Spirit

In a glen full of giggles, a spirit takes flight,
Who trips on a root that was peeking in fright.
With leaves in her hair, she starts to pirouette,
And twirls through the forest without any fret.

A raccoon joins in with a hat full of snacks,
He juggles some berries, the spirit relax.
While fungi discuss their most fascinating tales,
Of toadstools and mushrooms, with whimsical gales.

A parade of odd critters now leads the way,
With frogs in tuxedos who leap and who play.
The spirit just laughs, and the forest replies,
With blossoms like streamers, a natural surprise!

Through realms of enchantment, mischief will thrive,
Together we'll wander, feel oh so alive.
With whimsy and joy wrapped in mossy delight,
Nature's our playground, where humor shines bright!

A Path Paved with Gold and Green

In the woods where squirrels plot,
I tripped on roots and ducked a shot.
Heard a rustle, saw a hat,
Thought it's wisdom—just a cat!

Dandelions danced in the breeze,
A tangle of laughter, oh, if you please!
I posed as a tree, tall and grand,
Until I fell—now that was planned!

Mushrooms giggled, hinting delight,
As I stumbled through the bright daylight.
With every slip, the forest cheered,
Now who's the fool? Oh, how I've steered!

Golden rays tickle the ground,
In this merry chase, joy's abound!
Tall tales grow taller with each tree,
Watch out for leaves—oh, they got me!

Threads of Yesterday

Tangled fibers of tales we weave,
A tapestry of summers, I believe.
A critter scuttled, what a sight!
Dressed in leaves, lost in twilight!

I saw a squirrel in a suit,
Gossiping with a ghostly brute.
A picnic planned, snacks all around,
Oops! Someone's missing—where's the hound?

Memories flutter like paper kites,
While petals argue about their rights.
A whispered secret, a squawk, a flap,
Hey, was that a bird or just a nap?

Winding back through laughter and crumbs,
Under the snickers, the joy still hums.
Just follow the threads, they'll lead you right—
To a root beer float and a long fun night!

Mysteries Cradled by the Wild

Beneath the ferns, a riddle stirs,
A cheeky breeze reveals some purrs.
What shenanigans do shadows hold?
An acorn's tale that's yet untold!

Hiding beetles don little veils,
Conspiracies of woodland snails.
A bashful flash—a bunny's plight,
Danced off a tree, what a hefty sight!

Nuts in pockets, twigs in hair,
A wild affair, with woodland flair.
Duck, duck, goose, or was it deer?
Either way—grab a popsicle here!

The moon laughs softly at our plight,
As we tiptoe home, under starlit night.
Chasing tales, we wander on,
In a comedy where the wild is drawn!

Beneath a Tangle of Green Dreams

Beneath the branches, where shadows play,
  I lost my sandwich; it's gone astray!
A chipmunk giggles with crumbs in hand,
  Shrugging at me, 'This was the plan!'

  Dreaming of pies and sweet lemonade,
  Instead, it's ants that made the trade.
  With leafy hats, these critters can chat,
    As I tumble and roll in a leafy spat!

  A daisy wiggles—a dance for the bold,
    Daring drinkers from a cup of gold.
  Oh nature, you jest with every turn,
    In this garden of chaos, I still yearn!

  With laughter echoing in every nook,
    The woods are wiser than any book.
So join the march, leave troubles behind,
In the tangle of dreams, pure joy you'll find!

Ashes and Amber in a Forest's Embrace

In a woodland rich with cheer,
A squirrel wore a wig, oh dear!
He pranced around, a nutty king,
While trees laughed loud, their branches swing.

A fox in boots danced on a log,
Chasing shadows with a grin, the rogue!
With playful leaps and silly spins,
The forest sang, let the games begin!

But pinecones launched with epic flair,
As chipmunks cheered from their tiny lair.
A woodland feast of joy and jest,
In this embrace, they're all the best!

With whispers in the rustling leaves,
The silly tales, the forest weaves.
Through ashes and amber, glee ignites,
In nature's heart, the fun delights!

Shenanigans of a Leafy Realm

In a leafy realm where laughter grows,
The bunnies played with garden hose!
They watered flowers, danced spree,
While bees all buzzed a symphony.

An owl cracked jokes from the tallest tree,
As squirrels held a talent spree.
Who can dance, and who can sing?
The forest echoed with everything!

A chipmunk juggled acorns round,
While raccoons pulled pranks without a sound.
They stacked up leaves in a tower so high,
But down it came—oh my, oh my!

With giggles muffled in rustling grass,
The leafy realm was full of sass.
Amidst the fun, the mischiefs gleam,
In nature's antics, there's always a dream!

Paths of Illusion and Reality

On winding paths through shades of green,
   The hedgehogs spun, a funky scene.
   With a shuffle here and a belly roll,
They merged illusions with heart and soul.

   A rabbit claimed he could jump so high,
     But tripped on roots, oh me, oh my!
     Laughter echoed through the wood,
      As critters giggled, feeling good.

    A turtle strolled at a gentle pace,
    Bragging about his charming grace.
    Yet every time he took a stride,
  He'd trip on ferns—what a silly ride!

    In this maze of trickery and fun,
Where shadows dance, and friends outrun,
   Reality blends with laughter's call,
  And whimsical hearts will rule us all!

Hues of Melancholy in the Woods

In woods where hues of sadness blent,
A woeful tree felt slightly bent.
It knitted frowns with leaves a-sway,
But soon found joy in a silly play.

With branches stretched, it tickled the air,
While mushrooms giggled without a care.
A mopey toad began to croak,
And with each note, the gloom bespoke.

Yet from the roots, a sprout did rise,
A bursting bloom, with cheeky eyes.
It told a joke so wild and rare,
The forest laughed without despair!

Though often colors shift from light,
With laughter bright, they set things right.
For even when the mood seems dark,
The woods can spark that funny mark!

Beneath the Twisting Branches

Squirrels dance on branches high,
Chasing tails as time flies by.
A nut rolls down with quite a thud,
A splat in nature's leafy mud.

The wind whispers jokes to nearby trees,
Tickling leaves with a gentle breeze.
A grumpy owl gives a silly hoot,
As rabbits play in their funny suits.

Frogs leap high, then belly flop,
While butterflies perform a hop.
The acorns giggle, drop and roll,
In this funny forest stroll.

So join the fun beneath the sky,
Where nature's laughter will surely fly.
With every step, there's joy to find,
In this wild woodland, unconfined.

The Intersection of Time and Nature

Time ticked away, a funny face,
Nature blinked, made its case.
A clock, oh dear, with vine and moss,
Said, "Don't hurry, what a loss!"

Pinecones crunch beneath our feet,
Nature's rhythm, quite the beat.
What time is it? Who really cares?
In funny hats, we all wear flares!

Loud crickets chirp their silly song,
While daisies dance, they can't go wrong.
"Oh dear!" they sigh, "We're all quite bold,
Why grow up when we can unfold?"

So here we are, where time stands still,
With tree-bark laughter, there's much to thrill.
On paths of whimsy, here we sway,
In nature's playground, we'll dance and play.

An Ode to the Autumnal Whisper

Oh autumn comes with a golden wink,
Leaves scatter, twist, and dance, I think!
With each flutter, a giggle spills,
As pumpkins grin and do their drills.

Squirrels wear their jackets fine,
Stuffing nuts, oh, how divine!
The trees chuckle, their branches sway,
As autumn whispers, "Let's have a play!"

Wind carries tales of funny sights,
Of acorns rolling into fights.
The sun begins its soft retreat,
As we march on with jolly feet.

So toast to leaves with colors bright,
In this comical autumn light.
With laughter echoing through the woods,
We revel in our leafy moods.

The Heartbeat of Woodland Dreams

In the heart of woods where giggles bloom,
Hiding critters create a room.
An orchestra of rustling leaves,
Tickles your socks as nature weaves.

The owls crack jokes, wise and spry,
With a wink that makes the squirrels cry.
Foxes prance with their silly swag,
While frogs croak like a comedy rag.

A woodland stage where no one sleeps,
With laughter that the forest keeps.
In every beat, a story spins,
The dreams of trees and furry kin.

So listen close to the woodland cheer,
With every heartbeat, smiles appear.
In nature's laughter, we all find grace,
So let's join in this fun-filled space!

Echoing Footfalls on Crisp Ground

With each step, the crunch sounds loud,
Squirrels stare as if I'm a crowd.
They scurry up trees, quick as a wink,
While I ponder the meaning of this clink.

A chipmunk giggles, then puffs out its cheeks,
As I trip on a root, oh how the ground squeaks!
Nature's watching, with a twinkle of glee,
As I weave through the trees, quite clumsily.

The breeze gives a chuckle, a playful tease,
Whispers of laughter flutter like leaves.
I chase after shadows, yet they slip away,
While I debate if I'm here to stay.

Oh, how the branches sway and bend,
Like a comical dance, never to end.
I laugh with the trees, they laugh back at me,
Footfalls echo wild, how funny can be!

The Colors of Remembrance

In hues of orange, I start to ponder,
Did I wear this jacket? Or was it a blunder?
The purple leaves swirl like dancers in flight,
I trip on a twig—what a glorious sight!

Yellow spots glow, my feet feel they're dreaming,
As the squirrels plot, or so it seems—scheming.
I take a step forward but a leaf and I clash,
A soft crispy snap, oh, quite the loud crash!

The world is a gallery; I'm just passing through,
In a coat of confusion, of colors askew.
Fallen foliage tickles my toes in delight,
While the sun winks down—a comical sight.

With a flick and a tumble, I roll down the hill,
Not quite the plan, but oh what a thrill!
The colors now swirl, like a painter's mad thrill,
In the forest's embrace, I'm abuzz, what a spill!

A Pilgrimage Through Nature's Archive

I wander past stories etched in each tree,
A squirrel's a scholar, who costs little fee.
With acorns for wisdom, it fills up my mind,
As I seek ancient trails, where giggles unwind.

The path is like candy, sweet twists and turns,
But I'm tripping and slipping, how nature discerns!
Each leaf holds a secret, a naughty old jest,
I laugh at my clumsiness and join their quest.

With every misstep, I'm peeking through time,
Inside this green library, chaos does rhyme.
A chatter of robins shares gossip galore,
While a beetle laughs loudly at my tumble and score.

Through history's pages, I prance like a fool,
Nature's my tutor, and she's breaking the rule.
So here in the wild, I'll embrace the absurd,
A pilgrimage muddied, but oh, how it stirred!

In the Silence of Fallen Shades

In quietude whispers, the leaves can conspire,
To weave tales of mischief, fuel dreams with their fire.
I wander in shadows, all wide-eyed and spry,
As giggles of nature float softly nearby.

A twig snaps beneath me—a comedic ballet,
While squirrels recline, laughing, "What's with this display?"
Amidst all the stillness, I'm barely composed,
A comical assembly where laughter is posed.

Each rustle a secret, each shadow a jest,
While I search for direction, I'm quite the odd guest.
The wind teases gently, urging me to play,
In the silence of shades, I've lost my own way!

A dance with the shadows—a frisky charade,
They wink and they wave, as if life's a parade.
In nature's embrace, hilarity's breed,
For those who stumble still plant laughter's seed!

The Stillness of Sunlit Glades

In a sunny spot, I sit so still,
Watching squirrels plot their next thrill.
One drops a nut, it bounces by,
I swear it winked, oh my, oh my!

A bunny hops, it gives a chortle,
While dancing around a half-eaten turtle.
The bugs wear shades; the sun is bright,
They gossip softly about who's in sight.

Mushrooms giggle beneath their caps,
They argue about their funny mishaps.
A leaf takes flight, a kite in disguise,
As I chuckle at these clever guys!

Yet in this place of whimsy and cheer,
I wonder if they're all sipping beer.
With nature's jest, they might just tease,
Life's a laugh in sunlit leaves!

Amidst the Rustling Canopy

Among the branches, whispers go,
Of trees that know what we don't know.
A parrot squawks, a voice so grand,
As if he's conducting a jungle band.

The wind plays tricks with my messy hair,
Down comes a feather from who knows where.
I try to catch it, but it floats on high,
And the trees just giggle as I stand by!

A scared raccoon darts from sight,
Did I just blink? Oh what a fright!
A butterfly flutters through the air,
Dancing like it doesn't have a care.

The canopy sways, laughing loud,
While the sun peeks in, feeling proud.
Nature's a joker, in its own right,
With stories to tell till the end of night!

Treading on Tapestries

With every step, I tread on art,
A carpet of colors, a nature's heart.
Pinecones scatter like marbles in play,
And laughter erupts with each little sway.

A clever snail with a judging gaze,
Is taking its time in this leafy maze.
I wave at a lizard, it pauses to stare,
'What's with the shoes? Not very fair!'

Beneath the ferns, a secret dance,
The toads in their finest, all in a trance.
Each footfall's a story, each twist a tale,
As the wind tells jokes while we set sail.

The earth's a jester, the trees its stage,
Every leaf a line in this quirky page.
So I laugh with the critters, join in the spree,
In this lush, green gallery, oh whimsy with glee!

Solitary Journey Between the Trees

On this solitary path, I roam,
With squirrels plotting their acorn dome.
A branch just waved, or was it my mind?
The trees chuckle softly, oh how unkind!

An owl hoots from its lofty perch,
It seems to judge my gentle lurch.
I swear it rolled its eyes, then sighed,
As I tripped over roots that no one spied.

The shadows play games, hide and seek,
While a chipmunk pauses to critique.
"What's in your pocket?" it boldly demands,
"I swear it's just snacks, not treasure from lands!"

Yet here I wander, a jester's fool,
Among the woodland, my secret school.
With chuckles and giggles, it's easy to see,
This journey's a comedy, wild and free!

A Heart Hidden in Green

In a jungle of foliage, I go,
Tripping over roots, oh what a show!
A squirrel steals my sandwich with glee,
Laughing at me from atop a tree.

The grass tickles my nose as I sneeze,
While butterflies dance, doing as they please.
I shout, 'Hey, that's my drink, you silly bee!'
But it buzzes away, so carefree, you see.

When branches knock hats to the ground,
I wonder how many lost treasures I've found.
Nature's a jester, so full of surprise,
With each little mishap, I can't help but rise.

So I stroll through the woods with comedic flair,
In this leafy realm, I shed every care.
If laughter is golden, then I'm draped in gems,
Finding joy in the arms of these leafy friends.

The Weight of Amber Memories

I stumbled on sticks that creaked like old men,
Hiding secrets of summers back then.
Amber leaves float like memories missed,
Each one a giggle, a hug, or a tryst.

I skip through the piles, and oh, what a sight!
A dog darts past me, all furry and bright.
He jumps in the leaves, with no care at all,
Laughing at gravity—oh how we both fall!

I recall silly dances with mushrooms and ferns,
Tripping and twirling, as laughter returns.
The wind gives a chuckle, joins in my glee,
While the trees nod along, as if in decree.

My pockets are filled with the weight of it all,
The stories of breezes, the sound of a call.
So let's gather our joy, let it splash and swirl,
In this amber wonder, let laughter unfurl.

Roots of Reflection

Beneath the old oak, where shadows droll,
I ponder my life, but then lose control.
With bugs on my back and leaves in my hair,
I wonder if wisdom needs more than a chair.

Roots spread like secrets, entwined oh so tight,
Holding the tales of my laughable plight.
I trip on my thoughts, as they scatter like seeds,
While squirrels giggle at my misadventurous needs.

The sun peeks through branches, a spotlight of fun,
But my glasses are missing, so I squint in the sun.
Nature's a mirror, reflecting my face,
With dirt on my shirt, I embrace my own grace.

So here in the wild, I'm anchored and free,
Each chuckle a branch in this tall, wise tree.
With roots full of lessons and leaves full of laughs,
I'm a jester on earth, in a world full of gaffs.

When the Breeze Whispers Softly

The breeze whispers secrets as I stroll through the glade,
Tickling my ears like a playful charade.
I giggle and dance as it tousles my hair,
Each gust feels like nature's own loving affair.

With chimes in the branches, their bells softly ring,
I feel like a queen in this land of spring.
A toad croaks a joke, and I snicker aloud,
In this comedy hour, I feel quite proud.

The wind blows a riddle, and leaves twist and turn,
While my heart gives a leap, for laughter I yearn.
A parade of pink petals spins down in the air,
Spreading joy like confetti with a whimsical flair.

So I follow the breeze, with my head held up high,
This whimsical journey, oh how time flies by!
With each fleeting moment, I savor the play,
Nature's own laughter, carrying me away.

The Silence Between the Boughs

In whispers soft, the branches sway,
They giggle at squirrels who boldly play.
A little bird sings an off-key tune,
While shadows dance 'neath the smiling moon.

The leaves are gossiping, who would have guessed?
They plot and scheme, oh what a test!
A critter sneezes, a leaf flies high,
While the owl hoots out a sleepy sigh.

A mushroom winks from its cozy spot,
It's quite the show, this leaf-strewn plot.
The wind takes bets on who'll be the prank
In this leafy realm, where all giggle and clank.

Beneath the boughs, the laughter grows,
As the ants file by in neat little rows.
"Oh, what a party!" cries out the breeze,
"We've thoroughly lost all sense of degrees!"

In the Heart of the Wilderness

In the wild woods where chaos reigns,
A bear stumbles on his own shoelaces' chains.
Raccoons in masks sneak off with a pie,
While the deer stop mid-step to ask, "Oh my!"

Frogs croak like they're part of a band,
As hedgehogs throw leaves, it's quite unplanned.
The sun peeks through, just in time to see,
A chipmunk juggle three acorns with glee.

The trees crack jokes that only they know,
While the grumpy old rock starts out slow.
But soon with a chuckle, down rolls a stone,
It joins in the fun, never to moan.

In this wild space, time dances and plays,
With merriment spun in whimsical ways.
So hurry on down, don't forget your hat,
Or you might just miss the playful old cat!

A Kaleidoscope of Nature's Disguise

A chameleon dons a rainbow coat,
He struts down the path like a sassy goat.
The flowers all chuckle, "You look quite grand!"
While butterflies flutter, brigade all planned.

In every hue, a tiny ant strays,
Wearing a leaf like it's haute couture phase.
"Check me out," he declares with delight,
As clovers applaud from their spots out of sight.

The sunflowers spin tales of their height,
While pumpkins debate who's got the best fright.
"Just look at my stem!" cries a gourd in the crowd,
It's amidst laughter, going terribly loud.

A breeze decides it's time for a whirl,
Sending all petals into a twirl.
In this crazy scene, let laughter abound,
Nature's a show, with silly all around!

The Flight of Autumn's Breath

With a whoosh and a giggle, the wind takes flight,
It sweeps all the colors into pure delight.
Pumpkins roll round like they're late for a date,
As leaves spin about, they just can't wait.

An acorn narrates a tall tale so wild,
Of squirrels and their dreams, each time they are styled.
"I'm not just a nut!" it puffs up with pride,
While saplings stand guard, with no place to hide.

Crisp air is filled with the sound of pure fun,
As the geese honk loud, "Hey, is that everyone?"
They flap their wings, challenging the breeze,
In a race that mixes with giggles and wheeze.

Let's celebrate autumn in chuckles and cheer,
For nature's our canvas, with laughter so near.
And if you find joy in this autumn's mess,
You'll dance with the leaves in their playful dress!

Beneath the Treetops' Embrace

In the shade where the squirrels tease,
I tripped on roots and fell with ease.
A bird laughed loud, I blushed and stared,
My lunch now gone, the critters dared.

I waved at leaves, they waved right back,
A breeze swooshed in, I lost my snack.
With acorns flying, a fun-filled spree,
The trees conspired to laugh at me.

I danced a jig, they spun around,
With branches tall, I felt so bound.
Yet acorns dropped, a clumsy rain,
Just nature's way to share my pain.

Underneath the boughs, for giggles' sake,
A leafy tango, my knees now ache.
With every step, a twist or turn,
In this green riddle, I still must learn.

Wandering Through the Foliage

I wandered in and lost my map,
A leaf hit me, what a slap!
Giggles rose from the nearby trees,
They said, "Come play, we aim to please."

With branches low, I ducked and dove,
A pinecone landed, oh, what a trove!
My hat flew high, what a funny sight,
As nature laughed at my little plight.

I asked a twig for help, no sound,
Just leaves a-rustle, all around.
In the shrubbery, my friend, the bug,
Offered me a seat, a cozy rug.

Through every twist of nature's cheer,
I danced like no one was even near.
With laughter echoing through the green,
The trees rejoiced, a funny scene.

Fragments of an Emerald Dream

Amid the green, so bright and bold,
I met a gnome, with tales retold.
His mushroom cap was quite askew,
He chuckled hard, I laughed too.

With riddles tossed like pinecone bombs,
He lured me in with leafy charms.
I spun around, my feet went wild,
Nature's whim turned me to a child.

In the mist, I found a toad,
He croaked a song, my funny ode.
His froggy stance and quirky hop,
With every leap, I couldn't stop.

In emerald dreams, we made our fray,
With gnomes and frogs, the silliest play.
As branches waved, I joined the dance,
In nature's grip, I took a chance.

The Mahogany Maze

In a maze of mahogany, oh so fine,
I lost my thoughts, tripped on a vine.
A raccoon peeked, with mischief in eyes,
And in the laughter, my worries disguise.

I turned a corner, met a big tree,
It scratched my back, said, "Just let it be!"
With whispers soft, they sang to me,
In this maze of laughter, I wandered free.

A squirrel called out, "This way, come on!"
But every step turned into a con.
A dance-off started, leaves as my guide,
Two-step in the woods, nature's pride.

With mahogany shades and joyous glee,
I twisted and twirled, they followed me.
In the laughs of the maze, I found my groove,
A fabulous rhythm that made me move.

www.ingramcontent.com/pod-product-compliance
Lightning Source LLC
Chambersburg PA
CBHW071842160426
43209CB00003B/388